Princess Liliokalani
Does Not Believe in Racism & Hate Crimes Because She is Colorblind

Dr. Herbert K. Naito

Copyright © 2024 Dr. Herbert K. Naito

ISBN (Paperback): 979-8-89381-080-6
ISBN (eBook): 979-8-89381-081-3

All rights reserved. No part of this book may be reproduced
or transmitted in any form or by any means, electronic or mechanical, including photocopying,
recording, or by any information storage and retrieval system, without permission
in writing from the copyright owner.

The views expressed in this work are solely those of the
author and do not necessarily reflect the views of the publisher, and the
publisher hereby disclaims any responsibility for them.

508 West 26th Street KEARNEY, NE 68848
402-819-3224
info@medialiteraryexcellence.com

Table of Contents

Chapter 1 1

Chapter 2 27

Chapter 3 31

Chapter 4 41

Summary 43

The US Review of Books 50

Something About The Author

He is a graduate of the University of Northern Colorado with a BA and MA degrees in biological sciences and with a certified teaching certificate in secondary education in Colorado. He also has a PhD degree in physiology from Iowa State University and a Master's degree in business administration from Lake Erie College. He was a Clinical Professor of Clinical Chemistry at Cleveland State University Graduate School of Chemistry (And board certified) and Clinical Associate Professor at the Ohio State University School of Medicine.

He served on the medical staff at The Cleveland Clinic Foundation as a Senior Scientist and published over 150 peer-reviewed scientific papers in medicine. He was also on the medical staff at the Department of Veteran's Affairs in Cleveland, Ohio as Head of Clinical Chemistry and Point-of-Care testing. He is current on the Board of Directors at the Mercy Health Foundation in Youngstown, Ohio.

He was invited to Who's Who in the Midwest, Who's Who in America, Who's Who in Frontiers of Science and Technology, Who's Who in Society, Who among Asian-Americans, Who's Who in Science, Who's Who in

Science and Engineering, and Who's Who of the year. He is also listed in American Men and Women of the year, American Biographical Institute (ABI) Most Admired Men and Women of the Year, ABI Most Admired Man of the Decade, International Biographical Center (IBC) International Man of the Year, IBC international Man of the Year, IBC International Who's Who of Intellectuals, ABI Five-Hundred Leaders of Influence, National Association of Distinguished Professionals, and Covington Who's Who Top Executive of the Year.

He is a third-generation Japanese American that was born and raised in Hawaii-an international-multicultural community. He gave lectures in every corner of the world on heart disease, which gave him the opportunity to observe and study how people of different skin colors get along with one another. This book is dedicated to all children who seek a peaceful and safe life. More of our children are entering the work force (part-time or fulltime) at an earlier age and are being exposed to our violent society. We need to protect them in every way possible.

This book was supported by a generous grant from the Dr. and Mrs. Herbert K. Naito Charitable Foundation.

Chapter 1

Hawaii—The Melting Pot of The Nation—Has The Least Amount of Hate Crimes & Gun Violences

Aloha, my name is **Princess Liliokalani (Lily-o-ka-lani)**; I was born and raised in Hawaii where very little hate crimes occur because it is the melting pot of the nation where people live in peace and harmony. I am a hapa—Hawaiian word for mixed breed—10% Chinese heritage, 20% Japanese heritage, 40% Caucasian heritage, and 10% Hawaiian Heritage. Scholars and sociologist claim that if you want to experience to Hawaii, which is the most multi-cultural state in the nation. Caucasians or White Americans comprises the largest racial/ethnic group (40%) in Hawaii, followed by the Pilipino-Americans (25%), Japanese Americans (20%), Chinese Americans (10%), others (5%). What is different in Hawaii is 25% of the Hawaiian residents are mixed with more than one race; Alaska has the next most Asian-American subgroup with 7%.

Photo 1. *Princess Liliokalani is a true-blooded Hawaiian (Hapa or mixed breed with 40% Caucasian-American, 25% Philipino-American, 20% Japanese-American, 10% Chinese-American, 5% Other nationalities).*

What does RACISM mean to you? The dictionary defines it as a belief that some races are superior to others –whereby discrimination, prejudices, and hate crimes exist.

According to the United Nations and Human-Rights Network, people are treated ***differently***.

Why?

Is it because of their skin color?

Just take a look at the skin. It is only one layer thick—the thickness of a sheet of tissue paper—that's all; so, what is the bid deal about skin color? We should view skin color as beautiful. In fact, why do we spend so much money making or colorless skin darker with suntan lotions—to have darker skin color (Photo 20)? Can you explain that to me why people of color are discriminated or treated with hate crimes?

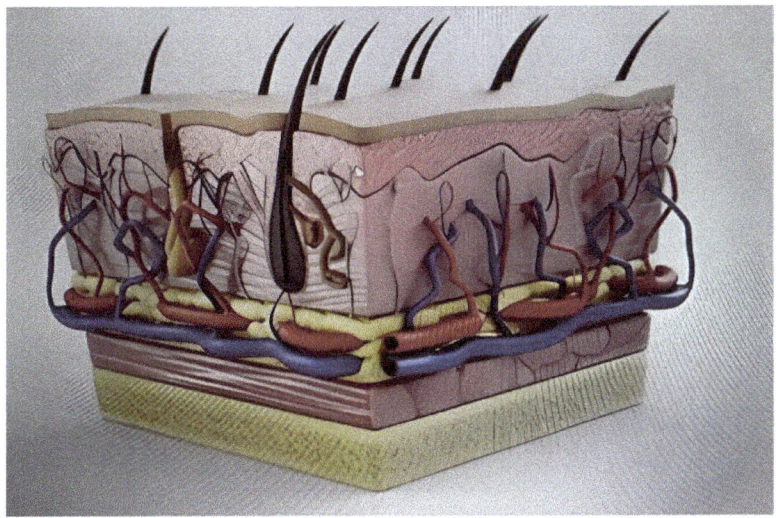

Photo 2. Anatomy of the skin. The pigmentation of the skin color is only one layer thick (The thickness of one sheet of paper). Beneath that one layer of color, we are basically the same. Just our attitudes, knowledge, thinking processes, feelings, and the like are different.

Photo 3. This white young girl is getting a suntan during the Winter to get some color which will make her look healthier and more attractive.

Is it because of their different culture and different dressing styles? Why don't you like this presentation of a beautiful kimono celebrating a traditional tea ceremony?

Photo 4. Is it because their culture is different when they sit on the floor to celebrate the traditional Japanese-tea ceremony?

Photo 5. Or is it because the Arabic culture dresses differently and look different from you?

Is it because of the different languages that they use are different from yours? Why should the sounding of different cultural languages offend you? Is it the content of the language that disturbs you?

Photo 6. Is it because the different religion used by the Orthodox Jewish people?

Is it because of the different ways that they dress or look? Why do you criticize how other children look? Do you feel that the way you dress and look warrant a negative statement? Or would this world be a better place to live if we all had a ***positive*** attitude or a ***negative*** attitude? Your mind is a very powerful tool; why not think with *pride, joy, love, empathy, happiness, pride, joy, faith?* Instead of *hate regret, fear, sadness, shame, anger, guilt?*

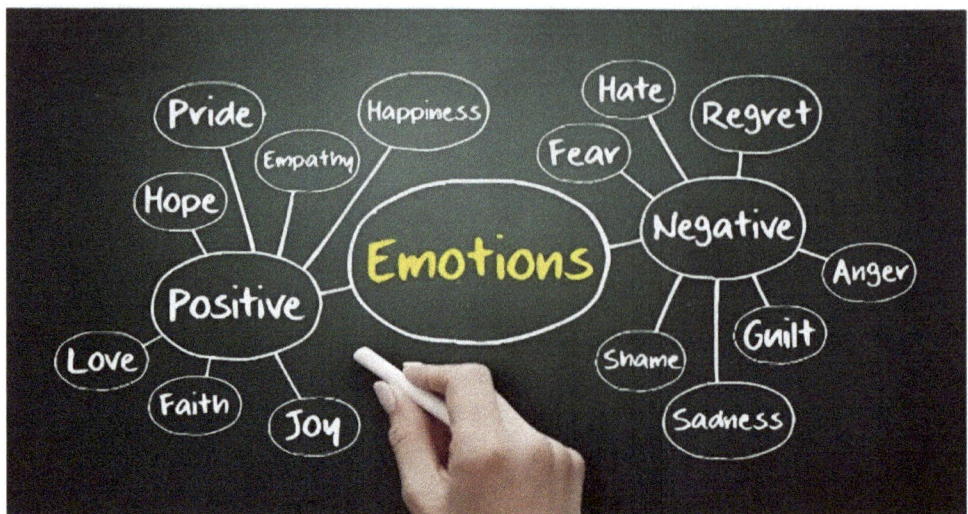

Photo 7. You have a choice of thinking POSITIVE or NEGATIVE thoughts. Why not think Positive instead of Negative? Hate crimes are derived from negative thoughts.

Photo 8. Is it because this beautiful Chinese American girl looks different? This is Stephanie Lee who was Miss Chinatown San Francisco, CA. She practices good human behaviors by not letting the teasing get under her skin and by being loving, kind, thoughtful, and giving to the hateful people.

During these hateful times we need to learn and practice respectful human behaviors to not incite racism and practice anti-hateful crimes.

Photo 9. Is it because the Japanese-American girl looks different?

Is it because of the different foods that they eat that you don't care for them? Why is so difficult for you to accept? Does everybody accept you all the time when you eat certain cultural foods that you love? Should there be a good reason for a hate crime to occur just because a person hates the food or the color of your eyes?

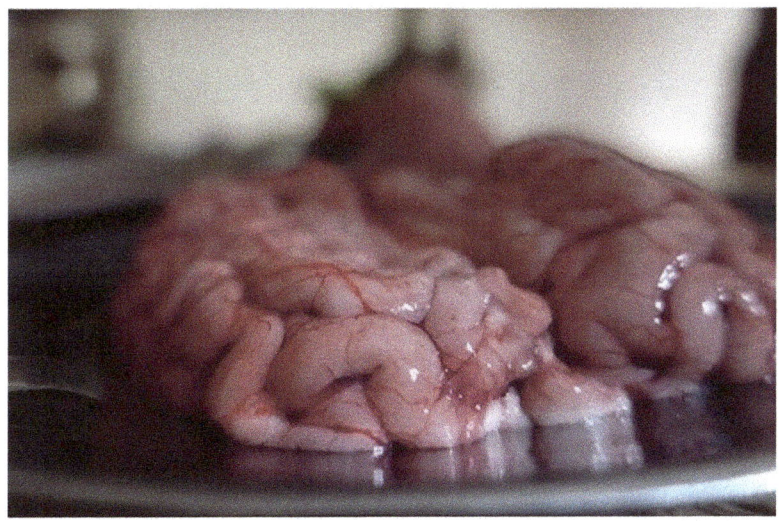

Photo 10. Is it because certain cultures eat foods that appear to be distasteful?

Is it because they speak a different language? Or because you simply don't understand what they are saying to you? Is it because you want to hear the English language? Many find the French or Italian language to be romantic.

Why can't you be more flexible?

Since there was no writing in ancient Hawaii, the role that the spoken Hawaiian language played in the daily life of ancient Hawaiians was huge. The Hawaiian language guided every facet and detail of their world. Chants and prayers were part of most every activity in the course of a day. From fishing to farming to eating to building and medicine, the language was used with much *mana (Spirit or power)* to bring about wellbeing and balance. Maybe that is part of the reason why there is so little lack of sharing, discrimination, racism, and violent crimes in Hawaii. Take a detailed examination at the language in the form of their proverbs:

- *Aloha Aku No, Aloha Mai No*—"I give my love to you, you give your love to me"

- *'A 'ohe loa I ka hana a ke aloha*—"Distance is ignored by love"

- *He 'olina lea ka ke aloha*—"Joy is in the voice of love"

- *Noho me ka hau 'oli*—"Be happy"

- *'A 'ohe lokomaika 'I I nele ke pana 'I*—"No kind deed has ever lacked its reward"

- *Ua Kuluma Ke Kanaka I Ke Aloha*—"It is natural for people to behave in a loving way"

- *Ku' ia Kahele Aka na'nu Ha' Aha's*—"A humble person walks carefully so as not *to hurt others*"

- *E hele me ka pu'olo*—"Always take an offering with you. • Make every person's place or condition better than you left it always"

- *Ho' ohanohano*—"Honor the dignity of others. Conduct yourself with distinction, and cultivate respectfulness"

- *Pono*—"The value of integrity, of rightness, and balance. The feeling of contentment when all is good and all is right"

- *Nana I Ke Kumu*—"Look to your sense of place and source of spirit, and you to find your truth"

One of the things that you do *NOT* want to do is "to harm with hate in mind." It is the Hawaiian Code of Forgiveness; It is important because when we forgive, who are we forgiving? Ourselves, of course. There are four simple steps:

• *Ponopono*—"Repentance"

• *Ho'oponopono*—"Forgiveness"

• *Mahalo Ke Akua*—"Gratitude"

• *Aloha Nui Loa*—"Love"

Photo 11. These close friends are a mixture of race, religion, and color.

Photo 12. Is it because this Japanese-American girl looks different?

*Photo 13. Is it because this Korean-American male looks different? Why does it offend you when a person is **different**? Why can't you treat that same person like your long-lost friend? Would you go out of your way to make her your best friend?*

Why is it so difficult to live peacefully together in harmony? Wouldn't you rather have friends that are kind, peaceful, warm, and helpful? Rather than hateful, mean, and cruel?

Photo 14. What kind of emotions run through your brain when you experience racism and hate crimes? Look at these children; they are all happy being friends.

Photo 15. The Japanese Empire mounted a sneak attack on Pearl Harbor on Sunday, December 7, 1941, at 7:55 A.M. on the island of Oahu, Hawaii. Most of the sailors attended church services at that hour. All Hell broke loose!

Let me select just one race as an example to show you how it can cause racism and hate crimes. Japanese-Americans immigrated from Japan to the United States over 130 years ago to find work and live peacefully with the

Americans. However, when Japan attacked Pearl Harbor in Hawaii on December 7, 1941, all Hell broke out. The Japanese-American citizens were corralled like cattle and thrown into internment camps that were barbed wire camps with towers with U.S. solders with machine guns to prevent any Japanese-American prisoners from escaping. The relocation of the Japanese-American Citizens meant that they lost property, homes, businesses; they could only bring with them whatever they could carry to the internment camp. The 10 barracks that were built were uninsulated and without hot-running water: For three-years they lived like that. They were not fully compensated for their hardship. However, after WW-II, Senator Daniel Inouye, struggled in Congress to obtain $25,000 for their hardship, never able to acquire their lost businesses or large mansions that they had before the War.

Photo 16. *Internment camp (A kind word for concentration camp) where the Japanese Americans were thrown in prison and locked up and guarded in a barbed-wire fence under the watchful eye of an American soldier with a machine gun 24/7 to prevent their escape.*

- Pinedale, California
- Pomona, California
- Tule Lake Internment Camp, California
- Topaz Internment Camp, Central Utah
- Gila River Internment Camp, Phoenix, Arizona
- Rohwer Internment Camp, Arkansas
- Heart Mountain, Wyoming
- Granada (Amache), Colorado
- Jerome, Arkansas
- Minidoka Internment Camp, Idaho

*Photo 17. Inside view a; notice the construction between the walls is **NOT** insulated—which makes it bitter cold during the Winter in Colorado, Idaho, California, and Wyoming—making living conditions extremely harsh. Additionally, there was **NO** hot- water for bathing or furnace for warm air during the Winter for comfort.*

Much of the food provided at the concentration camps to the Japanese American prisoners were unfit to eat. The cold winters were unbearable because the barracks were uninsulated, there were no blankets for warmth, and there were not heaters in the huts. Water was brought out in old buckets. Mail was sporadic and there were no current newspapers. Many elderly men and women died because of the poor living conditions, poor health because of the unhealthy food provided and the lack of exercise. The barracks were built quickly without insulation or heat for the Winter cold; neither was there running water (Hot or cold). The Humane Society of America would say that the shelter was unfit for their pets. The dignity of the Japanese-American citizen prisoners was less than honorable.

Photo 18. Freedom in America is certainly not free; however, the Constitution of the United States guarantee that we are born free.

Some of the predominant values held in the Japanese-American family are:

• Cleanliness

• Harmony

• Politeness

• Respect

• Formality

• Kindness

None of that came easy to the Japanese-American family. One thing that they did not lose track of was the importance of education. The mother of the Japanese-American family was responsible for ensuring that the children did their homework. Education in the Japanese-American household was a very high priority and the children understood that to the point whereby if they did not get into college or a private university, that meant 'loosing face' to the parents, close relatives and friends—committing suicide was uncommon. During 2010 the percentage that graduated with at least a Bachelor's degree are as follows:

• Asian-Americans   50%

• White-Americans   31%

• Black-Americans   18%

- Pacific-Islander-Americans   15%
- Hispanic-Americans   13%

Hate crimes are complex and there are many, many causes—education may be one of the helpful solutions that can help prevent racism by learning about anti-racism—again, be mindful that it is a *LEARNED* behavior from others, especially from parents, relatives, and friends.

Photo 19. An Asian-American mom is helping her daughter do her homework. Asian parents generally spend time with their children studding because of the higher scholastic achievement scores attained in school.

There is some evidence that having higher education may help with antiracism:

- The appearance of the ethnic group
- The parental upbringing of the child
- Violent gangs in the streets
- The History of crimes in the city streets
- Availability of guns in the streets
- Jealousy and envy of a given culture
- Different facial looks and physical appearances and attributes• Role of religion in the upbringing

Photo 20. A hearing handicap child that is learning sign language because she is being teased due to her hearing disabilities; which causes hate crimes because they are different.

Photo 21. A body with a handicap is always a target for teasing and taunting for the same reasons children with a handicap is considered less than normal and are considered targets for discrimination and hate crimes.

The attack on Pearl Harbor affected the United States in a profound way by the losses:

- 2,403 Americans died
- 1,143 Americans wounded
- 8 battleships destroyed
- 30 destroyers destroyed
- 5 submarines destroyed

- 3 US cost-guards destroyed
- 390 U.S. aircrafts destroyed
- 6 U.S. aircraft carriers destroyed
- 103 American civilians killed or wounded
- 1 Army aircraft shot down
- 3 one-man submarines destroyed

Photo 22. The Japanese Zero attack bomber attacked the Wahiawa Army Air field (in the middle of the island of Oahu) when Pearl Harbor was attacked.

Photo 23. Two Japanese Zero Torpedo Dive Bombers going to the Kaneohe Bay U.S. Naval station (Opposite the Pearl Harbor location) on the other end of the island to attack the docked U.S. battle ships and submarines.

Photo 24. Most Americans do not know about the fierce battle that took place on the opposite end of the island of Oahu when Pearl Harbor was attacked on December 7, 1941 at 7:59. The simultaneous attack at the Kaneohe U.S. Naval base was carefully planned to destroy more U.S. battleships.

These loses inflamed the American public. All the good that the Japanese-American citizens brought to the United States was totally erased. The racism and discrimination against the Japanese-American citizens were so bad that the Chinese-American citizens had to have painted signs on their backs, "I'm Chinese American" to protect themselves from hate crimes that were been inflicted on Japanese-American citizens. The Japanese-American citizens that served time in the concentration internment camps were persecuted even more; "We don't want Japs; Japs go home; We hate Japs." These hate crimes were perpetrated throughout the United States-especially along the California-Oregon coastline like shown below.

Photo 25. "Japs Keep Moving. This is a White Man's Neighborhood." Do you think that this is the height of human cruelty and outward documentation of hate at a maximum?

Where do the Japanese-American citizens go? America *is* their home! Just put yourself in their shoes! How would you feel if Americans told you that? There were over 246,900 hate crimes reported in 2020; but who were the perpetrators? There is one of the examples of White Supremist doing hate crimes. Recently, the FBI arrested 31 men from The Prominent Patriot Front White Supremist group for planning to incite a riot in Idaho on June 12, 2020.

- The White Supremist
- Black Americans
- Hispanic Americans
- Religion (Anti-Semitism)

Has anyone informed you about the United States 100th Army Infantry and the 442nd Battalion? The Japanese-American men were not allowed to enlist into the WW II because of their ancestry and they were given a 4-C status — unsuitable for service because of race or ancestry. On March 31, 1942, the nisei (2nd generation Japanese-American citizens) expressly forbidden from being inducted into the US armed forces. They petitioned to Congress that they should be allowed to defend the United States of America because they were American citizens. On February 1, 1943, President Ted Roosevelt announced the formation of the 442ⁿᵈ Regimental Combat Team—an allJapanese American unit made up of nisei men. An estimated 33,000 nisei men served in the US Army, of which 800 gave up their lives in the war. My dad's brother gave up his life fighting in that war.

The 100ᵗʰ/442ⁿᵈ Infantry Regiment Unit became the most decorated unit in US military history. The combat unit received 4,000 Purple Hearts, 21 Metals of Honor, and an unprecedented seven Presidential Unit Citations.

Photo 26. Part of the 100ᵗʰ/442ⁿᵈ All Hawaii Infantry Regiment Unit in Italy rescuing the Lost Texas Battalion that no other U.S. Military unit wanted to volunteer to help the All-Hawaii Company.

When my dad's brother was killed in Italy trying to save his fellow soldiers from the German army; did America appreciate the sacrifices that the majority that the Japanese- Americans gave?

Citizens gave during World-War II? Many Americans veterans still held grudges against Japanese immigrants and Japanese-American citizens. Along the West-coast line, prejudices, discriminations, and racism were ramped. How much more could the Japanese-Americans have done to prove their worth to America that they were true American citizens?

Photo 27. Enough is enough; it is time to stop Asian-American hate crimes. Can you imagine how that young girl really deep down inside?

Of all the groups of immigrants coming to the USA each year, Koreans are said to be among the most successful—many reaching the highest levels of achievement in this Country in a single generation. Many Korean immigrants settled in Los Angeles and in New York and went into business; nearly half opened their own business—like Korean import shops, green grocers, dry cleaning, finger nail salons. The language barrier prevented many Korean immigrants from getting decent jobs. Without that strong network of Koreans that helped each other, it has been much, much more difficult not only to gain access to an opportunity to make money, but also an opportunity to get capital to start a business. Koreans supported each other by pooling money to provide no-interest loans to help the newest immigrants start their businesses. The national trend has moved away from independently-owned business altogether. The East of Eden Grocery store on 79th and York Avenue is now a Chase Bank owned by Korean Americans.

The Korean population have a unique business model that they follow—called *keh*. This creative financial technique adapted from their homeland to help launch one of the most spectacular growths in small business creation of any American ethnic group in this century. Keh is a club in which Korean members contribute money each month, then wait for their turn to the recipient of the group pot of money.

It was not all peaches and cream with the Korean-American community in America. *The Korean American-African American Riots is an example:*

The 1992 Los Angeles riots were horrific. Looting and arson began on April 29, 1992. The result of several days of rioting, more than 50 people were killed, more than 2,300 were injured, and thousands were arrested.

About 1,100 buildings were damaged, and total property damage was about $1 billion, which made the riots one of the most-devastating civil disruptions in American history. This was sparked after a jury acquitted three Los Angeles police officers of use of excessive force for brutally beating Rodney King and failed to reach a verdict for a fourth officer. Included in that hate riots was the killing of Latasha Harling, a 15-year-old Black girl, by a Korean convenience store owner who said she stole a bottle of orange juice. The shop owner, Soon Ja Du, was sentenced to probation, community service and a $500 fine—a decision that was upheld a week before the uprising. Although many citizens of Los Angeles prided themselves on their city's ethnic diversity, many felt that the city's predominantly White police force practiced racial profiling and engaged in racist brutality against African Americans and Hispanic Americans. A videotape shot by a man who watched police officers brutally beat Rodney King to the ground failed, they clubbed him with their batons dozens of times. On April 29, 1992, protest and violence erupted almost immediately after the jury (Composed of 10 Whites, a Hispanic American, and an Asian American) acquitted the police officers of charges that included assault with a deadly weapon and excessive use of force. Hundreds of protesters congregated outside the LA Police Department chanting, "No Justice, No Peace." There was also large-scale rioting that resulted in 34 deaths in 1965. The live television coverage captured an assault on a White truck driver, who was pulled from the cab of his vehicle, beaten, and smashed with a cinder block. Reginald Denny, who was part of the news media, while trying to cover the news, made the incident more inflammatory with the kind of racial languages that were used. The news media must use restraint to minimize the sensationalism to obtain high viewer ratings. This is one of the areas where we can greatly improve controlling racism (See chapter 4). The news media need to restrain themselves by not sensationalizing themselves to keep the rioting down to a minimum. This is when "Black Lives Matter" movement started.

However, "Asian American Matters" too.

Actually, "All Lives Matter."

"All colors under the rainbow matter."

Why can't we conduct our lives as if we are ALL *"colorblind?"*

According to Eduardo Bonilla-Silva[1], most Whites in the United States rely on the ideology of color-blind racism to articulate their views, present their ideas, and interpret interactions with people of color. For example, they believe Black Americans are culturally deficient, welfare-dependent, and lazy. They regard affirmative action and reparation as tantamount to 'reverse discrimination.' Because Whites believe that they believe that discrimination is a thing of the past, minorities protestations about being racially profiled, experiencing discrimination in the housing and labor markets, and being discriminated against in restaurants, stores, and other setting are interpreted as 'excuses.' Following the color-blind script Whites support almost all the goals of the Civil Rights Movement in principle, but object in practice to almost all the policies that have been developed to make these goals a reality.

Although they abhor what they regard as Blacks' self-segregation, they do not have any problem with their own racial segregation because they do not see it as a rational phenomenon. Does every single White person subscribe to the frames, racial stories, and style associate with color-blind racism? The answer is obviously not. Historically, racial progress in America has always transpired because of the joint efforts of racial minorities and White progressive. No one can forget the courageous efforts of Whites such as John Brown, Taddeur Stevens, Charles Summer, Lydia Maria Child and the many Whites who joined the Civil Rights Movement—no one should ever ignore White militants who struggled for racial equality and who risked their lives for this goal. Therefore, today, as with yesterday, a portion of the White population is not singing the true tune of color blindness.

Black Americans for the most part, do not subscribe wholeheartedly to the frames of color blindness. Furthermore, Blacks have oppositional views on many important issues. For example, they believe discrimination is a central factor shaping their life chances in this Country, firmly support affirmative action, and are very clear about Whites' advantageous position in this society. However, some of the frames and ideas of color blindness have had a significant indirect effect on Blacks. For example, the frame of abstract liberalism has shaped the way many Blacks explain school and residential segregation. The style of color-blind racism has had very limited impact on blacks. Where Whites hesitated the use double-talk to state their views on racial matters, Blacks state their views clearly and without much hesitation, even when the discussion is interracial marriage. Only two of the four lines of color blindness have had some impact on some impact on Blacks.

Why being different can agitate the person next to you? Is it better that the planet be ALL aliens—all the SAME size, height, shape, color? What are the solutions to resolving discrimination, racism, prejudices?

Photo 28. Raw fish (Sashimi) eaten with sushi, which is made and served on special holidays in America. Before making any racial judgment, have your own children try eating sushi. It is delicious!

*Photo 29. **Kimchee:** This pickled vegetable is a favorite appetizer for Korean-Americans. It can be extremely spicey to match their hot temperament.*

Photo 30. ***Bullying:*** *This Asian-American girl looks different from other White-American children— so, she is being racially harassed.*

Photo 31. Everyone should experience everyday life like this three-year-old girl, who smiles every day, with joy and happiness. The outcome is every parent will be extremely elated.

How much are you willing to make friends with them instead to committing hate crimes because they are *different*? Are you willing to provide survival help by donating blankets, clothing, shoes, food? Are you willing to go a step further by providing shelter? Are you willing to shuttle them to the medical facilities because of their many illnesses? They may not even have the money or insurance to pay for the treatments.

Why should people's *differences* become problematic? Like your children eating vegetables and liking them, we need to train them early. Racism, hate crimes, and the like need to start as early as you can. Debra Van Ausdale and Joe R. Feagin[2] had the correct idea about educating children when they are young. I will have more to say on that important topic.

Photo 32. Of the 200,000 migrants that entered the U.S. from the Mexican border, the majority were from Mexico, Dominican Republic, Haiti, Honduras, El Salvador during 2020. Are you willing to be a hospitable family and adopt a family or provide them with necessities (food, fluids, blankets, shoes, clothing or even health-care insurance?).

Be mindful that they may be colored or even uncolored. Secondly, would you do this kind and benevolent gesture unconditionally? This is certainly a true act of kindness; we need more people in this world demonstrating this kind of behavior instead of hate.

Would you go so far as to provide healthcare; many immigrants have challenges with many illnesses and don't have monies for healthcare nor do they have insurances for treatments. Are you willing to go the extra mile and provide them shelter?

Influence of Being Different:

Why being different can agitate the person next to you? Is it better that the planet be filled with aliens—all the SAME size, height, shape, color? What are the solutions to resolving discrimination, racism, prejudices? What are your thoughts on helping the migrants? Should kindness, caring, and love be spread like peanut butter? Should there be any boundaries?

Why *differences* become problematic? Like your children eating vegetables and liking them, we need to train them early. Racism, hate crimes, and the like need to start as early as you can. Debra Van Ausdale and Joe R. Feagin[b] had the correct idea about educating children when they are young. I will have more to say on that important topic later.

Chapter 2

Science & Research in Racism should Predominate

We need more science and research on the causes of race and racism in America. Why is America the leading country when it comes to violent crimes in the schools, malls, stores, streets? Are we violent people by nature? Is it because we do not have adequate laws to protect our children?

Why don't we study countries with the least amount of deadly hate crimes? List of countries with the least racism in 2022

Countries	
Rank in the World	
Netherlands	
Canada	
New Zealand	
Sweden	
Denmark	
Finland	
Switzerland	
Norway	
Belgium	
Austria	
France	
Ireland	
Australia	

Ranked #1

Ranked #2

Ranked #3

Ranked #4

Ranked #5

Ranked #6

Ranked #7

Ranked #8

Ranked #9

Ranked #10

Ranked #11

Ranked #12

Ranked #13

According to the International Convention on the Elimination of all forms of Racial Discrimination (CERD) the United States is ranked 69th out of 78 countries. Why so much hatred and racism? We need to more research with the countries with the least racism are doing right. The hate crimes and racism must stop in America—*Now!* We must protect our precious resources—*OUR KIDS!* Look at what happened at Elementary School in Uvade, Texas. We need to build better protection plans including the elimination of semi-automatic weapons, double closed entrance doors with cameras, better arrest laws and gun laws and better mental health and stability screening.

Photo 33. AR-15 semi-automatic assault rifle that was designed and manufactured for wars and mass destruction. This was used in a public school in Uvalde, Texas; killed 19 children and two teachers! How would you feel if it was your best friend killed?

*Photo 34. This Phantom depicts the fact that we all seek **P-E-A-C-E** in this world, but there are still a lot of **EVIL**.*

Chapter 3

Causes and Solutions to Racism Bullying

I am adding this topic in this book because it is a common phenomenon that children experience in daily life which is part of hate crimes. Bullying seeks to harm, intimidate, or coerce someone perceived as vulnerable; it is a blustering, browbeating person especially one who is habitually cruel, insulting, or threatening to others who are weaker, smaller, or in some way vulnerable tormented by the neighborhood or school bully, a pimp, a hired ruffian, or sweetheart. Bullying is a repeated physical, social, or psychological behavior that refers to the misuse of power by a person or group towards another individual or person. It is totally unacceptable in the United States or any country. However, acts of bullying are typical for the educational institutions, especially in the high schools. The most prevalent age of bullying occurs between 11-13 years (33%), followed by 8-10 years (2150, teens (20%), 6-7 years (5%), and 4-5 years (1%). 2020 research shows that girls and boys are both victims and aggressors of bullying.

Why is bullying so harmful?

- What are the negative aspects and adverse consequences of bullying?

- What mental and physical trauma can be caused by bullying?

- What are the outcomes of bullying?

- What is the school environment and bullying policies like?

- What are the consequences of the bullying perpetrators and how are they treated?

- What do they do to the bystanders who watched the bullying?

- What kind of emotional and verbal aggressions are the perpetrators using?

- What kind of conduct does your friends and peers tolerate?

- Do you have a system in place that minimizes bullying?

- Does the social media contribute to the bulling?

Are anti-bullying programs effective? According to research, anti-bullying programs reduce school-bullying perpetration by about 20 percent. Do Federal anti-bulling laws? According to the Philippine government (RA 10627) the court decisions ruled in favor of the plaintiffs in only 2% of the cases. So, this is only an initial step in the process.

Cyberbullying can affect anyone and may even cost their life. Cyberbullying victims have suffered drastically from some types of cyberbullying. Cyberbullying victims are more likely to have low self-esteem, depression, and more likely to consider to consider suicide. Many young girls are forced to believe that society will not accept them unless their figure is identical to a model, changing their mentality to do unfortunate things toward their natural bodies. The social media has made it difficult for many young individuals to accept themselves for who they really are, and as a result it forces many of them to change themselves mentally and physically to be accepted to this changing society social media has been dreadfully created.

If you don't want to be bullied, don't do it to others. Go with the saying, "Do onto Others as You Want Others to do onto You." These are hateful crimes; remember Photo 6? You have choices—Positive or Negative. Making a person feeling crummy is not a good thing. Nothing good can come out of feeling bad. You want a photo showing smiles (Photo 14).

Photo 35. According to the latest research, one out of three children have been a victim of Bullying, which can truly be a hate crime. I truly don't understand why people even do it. Do YOU participate this kind of behavior?

Bullying can be done anywhere, anytime, even in the workplace. As more and more young kids enter the workforce (Part-time or full-time) more and more bullying and hate crimes will occur.

Case-Study #1: Ron works in a plumbing shop as an apprentice for six years and his boss, Eddie, called him gay and used offensive languages toward him. This is certainly an uncalled-for bullying and a hate crime filled with discrimination, prejudices, and racism, even.

Case-Study #2: Eddie even encouraged the other employees to call him names, asked him inappropriate questions and make crude insinuations about his personal life, which is uncalled for under any circumstances.

Case-Study #3: Eddie took his mobile phone and made him believe that he had posted inappropriate comments on a female friend's page. Do you believe that this is a case of bullying?

Case-Study #4: Eddie had one of his employees put a live mouse down the back of Ron's shirt. This is hateful but, is this a complaint for bullying?

Case-Study #5: Ron was too afraid to complain to his manager. Was that correct? What else could Ron have done? What would you do if you were Ron?

Ron took his case to the court and won under the Occupational Health and Safety Act 2004 and was awarded $12,500. The employees and Eddie were found guilty of risk in the workplace and workplace bullying.

To drive the point home on workplace bullying I will enforce it with another series of Case-Studies at a local bakery where they were required to perform tasks including baking, sandwich preparations, general food preparation, cleaning and delivery of orders to different businesses:

Case-Studies #A: The owner, Mike, the boss, was in the baking business for over 25 years and he had one assistant, Sam wo was a timid and quiet individual.

Case-Study #B: Over a two-year period, Sam was called "pig," "porky," "dog'" and other derogatory names by Mike, who occasionally yelled and threw a temper tantrum for no reason at all. How did that make you feel?

Case-Study #C: Sam was labelled as 'Useless' and 'a Waste of Space' by Mike. How did you sleep at night that evening?

Case-Study #D: Sam was told many times, "To go away and die; and die quietly." How did you feel when your friend picked you up to drive you home after work?

Case-Study # E: Sam went home a physical and mental wreck. Would feel the same way too? I know that I would feel horrible; however, I would say something!

Sam filed with the court and was awarded $50,000 under the Occupational Health and Safety Act 2004. The Judge told Mike to knock off the workplace bullying!

Carrying this hate crime further, I will go into racism. The causes of racism is multi-factorial—but it is a *learned* behavior—which should be stopped when your child is young; stopping racism and hate crimes the earlier the better. I am going to list a limited number of celebrities because I am not promoting them; I am trying to make a point about race and racism—it can happen anywhere, it can happen to anyone: rich or poor, White or Black, Jewish or Muslim, famous or not-so-famous. Do you recognize any of these people?

Name	
Race	
Affected by Racism	
Notible	
Worth	
Jenifer Lopez	

Puerto Rican-American	
X	
Actress Singer Grammy Emmy	
$400M	
Duches Meghan	
Multiracial	
X	
Actress	
$10	
Michelle Obama	
Multiracial	
X	
First Lady	
$70M	
John Legend	
Multiracial	
X	

Singer Grammy Academy
$45M
Thandie Newton
Multiracial
X
Actress Emmy
$14M
Lucy Liu
Chinese-American
X
Actress Emmy
$16M

Symptoms for Unforgiveness:

- You bring your anger and bitterness into every relationship.
- You become so wrapped up in the wrong that you cannot enjoy the present.
- You become depressed and anxious and cause hate crimes.
- You feel that your life lacks meaning or purpose, or that you're at odds with your spiritual beliefs.
- You lose the joy of Love for the Lord and for others.

A. There are Seven Steps to Forgiveness:

1. Acknowledge the hurt and anger that you have created to others.
2. Consider how the hurt and pain can affect you.
3. Accept that you cannot change the past, but you can change the present, and God can change the future.
4. Acknowledge how your wicked actions have hurt God—your savior.
5. Release yourself from the emotional prison and make a determination to forgive.
6. Repent.
7. Continue to pray to receive God's support and grace.

Photo 36. People of mixed colors, working together, harmoniously. This is the America we should all be striving for in the future. Aren't you anxious to experience this?

B. There are three types of Forgiveness:

1.Exoneration: essentially means that the slate is completely wiped cleaned and the relationship is fully restored to its previous sense of innocence. "To forgive and to forget."

2.Forbearance: this is a second level forgiveness, which is a partial forgiveness. It is an apology suggesting that the other person is partially to blame for the wrongdoing.

3.Release: this is the lowest level of forgiveness, which applies to situations in which the person who hurts you has never acknowledged any wrongdoing. He or she either never apologized or has offered an incomplete or insincere apology. Apology or not, no reparations have been given and the perpetrator has done little or nothing to improve the relationship:

"All bitterness, fury, anger, shouting, and reviling must be removed from you, along with all malice."

Ephesians 4:31-32

"When you stand to pray, forgive anyone against whom you have grievance, so that your heavenly Father may in turn forgive your transgressions.

Mark 11:25

"Then Peter came to Jesus and asked, 'Lord, how many times shall I forgive my brother or sister who sins against me? Up to seven times?' I tell you, not seven times, but seventy-seven times."

Mathew 18:21-22

The churches should take a more active role against anti-racism, antidiscrimination, and anti-prejudices by doing the following:

- Uniting with churches of other denominations; walk together hand-in-hand in the streets and pray together.

- Have printed materials and serve as a handout information.

- Ask the public to provide their opinions on how to curb racism.

- Get community leaders to provide Watch Blocks to be guardians of their community.

- Get guest speakers from countries (i.e., Netherlands, Canada, Australia) with the least amount of hate crimes to provide solutions to our violent gun crimes.

Photo 37. An Asian-American and a White-American are starting a life together. They will have outside challenges throughout their lives; however, they will overcome these circumstances with combined effort (husband and wife).

Photo 38. More and more mixed marriages should take place in America to reduce racism and hate crimes. For example, this couple will pass all their love to their child—which will take several generations to bare the fruit of the outcome of loving parents of mixed color. Has it ever passed your thoughts to experience a mixed marriage?

Chapter 4
Carrying a Concealed Weapon

Are you concerned that you may be shot by a hate crime shooter? You should be because the gun laws are going in the wrong direction. Beginning in January 1, 2023 the following states will allow residents in the following 25 states to carry a concealed weapon without a gun permit:

- Alabama
- Alaska
- Arizona
- Arkansas
- Georgia
- Idaho
- Indiana
- Iowa
- Kansas
- Kentucky
- Mississippi
- Missouri
- Montana
- New Hampshire
- North Dakota
- Ohio
- Oklahoma
- South Dakota
- Tennessee
- Texas
- Utah

- Vermont
- Wes Virginia
- Wyoming

Many American citizens, including myself, think the developing gun laws by Congress will not be adequate to protect our children. We will continue to have what happened at Robb Elementary School in Texas where 19 Hispanic children were gunned down. Notice that **Hawaii** is not among the list of 25 states to carry a concealed weapon without a permit. I firmly believe that this will help with curtailing the killing of children. We just have to do more to protect our precious children! Yesterday (June 12, 2022), 31 White Supremacist call the *Patriot Front* were arrested because they had planned to conduct a riot. I see no end in sight with these terror attacks.

Summary

Race and racism in America are a complicated multifactorial challenge; we certainly have to do better in controlling our children. We need to build better protection systems for our precious children. Our educational process needs improvement when it comes to reducing the hate crimes. Parents, teachers, and the community need to be educated along with our children. The local communities, like our churches, certain organizations (Boy Scouts of America, Girl Scouts of America, YMCA,) need to step in and participate more actively in educating our youths to be more considerate when it comes to race and racism and human lives. We need to change our attitudes by being more tolerant of color and non-color. We need to value life more and stop all the killings. Video gaming manufactures need to take greater responsibilities on their role of creating hate crimes by creating less violent characters. We need to learn new words like PEACE, HARMONY, COMPASSION, and LOVING ONE ANOTHER.

Photo. 39. Don't you hope and wish for every child in America to always be happy each day and every day?

*Photo 40. Isn't it about time we **STOP** Asian-American hate?*

*Photo 41. **FIST BUMP:** We need to show more physical friendship—especially between people of color—to eliminate or reduce racism and hate crimes and gun violence.*

Photo 42. **Holding Hands:** *If you desire to be friendlier to people of color (with their permission) or you have a personal relationship with a person of color—hold their hands—to demonstrate affection —to show how much you really care about people of color.*

Photo 43. According to the latest research, one out of three children have been a victim of bullying, which can truly be a hate crime—why even do it? Do YOU, do it? Why? What do you gain from it?

"New photo – I picked it myself."

Photo 44. Our united goal as good-hearted Americans is to LOVE one another, regardless of race, color, religion, creed, or ethnicity.

"New photo – I picked it myself."

*Photo 45. **Crown of Thorns:** Jesus Christ died for our sins—Racism and Hate Crimes –are sinful behaviors that must purged and eliminated from our body; instead, we must fill our heart with genuine **LOVE**.*

There are some key words you to tuck away in your noodle when you confront a racist or when a person is showing signs of wanting to participate as a hate crime perpetrator:

- Love
- Patience
- Do not demonstrate panic
- Be colorblind to the person
- Do not carry hate in your heart
- Be respectful to everyone
- Life is precious; do your part to protect all living beings
- Being colorblind may no longer fit into the empirical equation to prevent racism & hate crimes

*"Whether discrimination is
based on race
or creed or color
or land of origin,
it is utterly contrary to
American Ideals of
Democracy"*

President Harry S. Truman

Photo 45. The dove with the olive twig symbolizes PEACE & FRIENDSHIP: this should be our ultimate daily goal in life.

Notes

[←1]

Bonilla-Silva, Eduardo; Racism without Racists; Rowman & Littlefield Publishers, Inc.; Lanham, Maryland; 2003; 214 pages.

[←2]

Van Ausdale, Debra and Feagin, Joe R.; How Children Learn Race and Racism; Rowman and Littlefield Publishing Group, Inc; Lanham, MD; 2001, 240 pages.

Princess Liliokalani Does Not Believe in Racism and Hate Crimes Because She Is Colorblind

by Dr. Herbert K. Naito

book review by Barbara Bamberger Scott

"Why is it so difficult to live peacefully together in harmony?"

Author Dr. Naito has composed a vibrant treatise centered on issues of race and skin color and their potential effects on social behaviors, feelings, and legal issues. The setting for his artfully constructed work is Hawaii, where Naito was raised, noting that it is a state with a low number of hate crimes, providing a melting pot where people of all heritages live "in peace and harmony." The spokesperson for his salient points is the title's Princess Liliokalani, who initiates the book's themes by asking, "What does racism mean to you?" Is it, she questions, based on skin color (a thin layer that some people try to darken for greater beauty), dress styles, languages, foods, or other superficial elements?

The princess reminds readers of the treatment of Japanese American immigrants during World War II, making them a hated group, though many of them fought for America and had moved there to contribute their talents and skills to its culture and economy. Ther e is stress made as well on the prejudicial treatment of Blacks and others, bullying, cyberbullying, and the legality in some states of concealed weapons.

Naito is a highly qualified, internationally lauded, distinguished authority in the realms of chemistry and physiology and a third -generation Japanese American whose research regarding heart disease provided the basis for this remarkable book. He offers readers global data and history melded with simple, thought -provoking questions and declarations. He targets a wide range of readership, most especially dedicated to "all children who seek a peaceful and safe life." Brightly illustrated page by page with colorful contemporary and some black and white historical photographs, his book will offer insight to an international audience. By studying, discussing, and contemplating Naito' s forceful work, positive influences can be brought to bear and ameliorative changes made.

www.ingramcontent.com/pod-product-compliance
Lightning Source LLC
Chambersburg PA
CBHW042359030426

42337CB00032B/5154